Seller Finance UK

"Become the bank & profit like one"

By Paul Watts

ISBN: 1470038234
ISBN-13: 978-1470038236

DEDICATION

I dedicate this book to the millions of people suffering from the credit crunch. May you rise like the phoenix, out of the fire.

CONTENTS

1 - INTRODUCTION

Dear reader,

Thank you for buying my book. The year is 2011 and at the time of writing the UK consumer price index published by the Office of National Statistics has just topped 4.4% and the retail price index has crossed 5.1% this increases the pressure on the bank of England to raise its base rate of interest from the current record low of 0.5%

Despite most lenders having chosen to increase their profit margins rather than pass the interest rate reduction on to mortgage borrowers, there remains a substantial number of people whose mortgage lending is directly linked to the Bank of England Base Rate via tracker mortgages for example and these people have benefited.

The reduced range of mortgages and mortgage lenders in the market, exacerbating the effect of more stringent lending criteria are just some of the effects of the recession, nick - named the 'Credit Crunch' in the UK Market

If you have been living in the UK, since 2008 it would have been virtually impossible to avoid the news of the change in the property market.

Personally having lived in many countries I have been exposed to a lot of different ways of doing things, as a natural born entrepreneur, my passion has and always will be building businesses and I have been active in the property market for more than 8 years.

What I offer in this book are ways you can sell your home in any market; ways that perform especially well in a distressed market. When you chose to become 'The Bank' in the transaction, you can take control of the sale of your property. You will be in control of the finance and that makes a world of a difference.

The ideas, concepts and practices contained in this book are very, very old, in fact, thousands of years old. Before money, people engaged in trade and whenever the monetary systems collapsed, which throughout history has happened many times, people have *still* traded.

Barter is part of human nature, we naturally negotiate exchanges that don't involve any monetary element, none the less they still have a *value*. When the value exceeds that which can be immediately exchanged or there is a requirement to perform over time. Banking can be a wonderfully convenient system to facilitate transactions and lending, unfortunately banking is not always able to meet your needs and is not always available. With this background I present my take on Seller Financing.

Seller financing in its many variations is an exceptionally powerful strategy that can literally change your life.

Providing the financing for your buyer can enable you to sell your home when potential buyers are unable to get a mortgage, like in the current climate where banks have got problems of their own.

You can complete transactions much faster because there are fewer parties involved. Do you need to leave the country for a new job? Or take care of a sick relative?

Cash buyers do not require bank lending but there are fewer of them and because they are paying all cash they normally demand a significant discount and rightly so. Seller financing is a great way to provide yourself with a retirement income or a steady income for a family member.

Maybe you own a large home unencumbered, free and clear of any lending? You have retired and would prefer a smaller home? You want to downsize to a flat or small cottage in the country. Many people sell their home and invest the difference in stocks and shares (maybe with Bernie Madoff) for income in retirement. An alternative would be to sell your home with an element of seller financing, cover the cost of your new home with the deposit the buyer pays you. Then use the interest paid on the loan you provided the buyer, to deliver you a healthy income, secured on the home you just sold.

Seller financing allows for a very high level of creativity that is just not practical for a lending institution. You can develop a tailor made lending deal for yourself and the buyer that provides you with a much lower lending risk than banks have and even get a better return on your money.

What about your savings? The rate of return that you would get or are getting from a bank or building society is positively frail compared to what you would receive from seller financing your own home.

The distressing reality of current saving schemes is that you lose money. With many current plans paying a paltry interest rate of less than 1%, as I mentioned earlier, with the inflation rate at a hefty 4.4% currently, in real terms, you would end up with a negative savings plan.

Seller financing can easily outperform ISA's, Tessa's and most other typical investment funds and offers considerably more security. More importantly it is *guaranteed* by a property that you know very well, one you liked so much you bought it.

I hope you enjoy this book and that you digest the contents slowly giving yourself time to think of ways you can structure your own seller finance deals aided by the most powerful force in the universe, Compound Interest.

2 - WHAT IS SELLER FINANCE

Seller financing also known as owner financing, is probably the oldest form of financing there is.

The essence as I am sure you either know or you have guessed is that if you have something you want to sell, you allow the purchaser to pay you with installments, which is why seller financing is sometimes referred to as an installment contract.

One of the attractive attributes of seller financing is that between the two points A and B, A pays B everything else is flexible. As this book is intended for property transactions, let's focus on this area specifically.

If B owns a house and would like to sell that house, B can accept payments in stages. That is seller finance. THAT'S IT!

That is it in its most basic form but now, we must consider the multitude of choices E.g., How many payments? Over how long a period of time? How much interest do you choose to charge?

Of course most people would prefer to have all of their money now, but not all people.

Naturally, a bird in the hand (cash now) is worth more than two in the bush, as you can eat your bird (and spend your cash) now. If you do not eat your bird soon it will spoil, even if it is in the fridge, just as if you do not spend your cash inflation will eat it for you.

So, two birds in the bush stay fresher longer, however, you might not be able to eat them when you want to. If your cash is out as a seller finance loan, you can charge interest and your money will grow (the birds in the bush staying fresher longer) but you may not be able to collect all of your payments (your birds could fly away).

When you create a good seller financing structure, you automatically earn more money than in a straight sale and receive payment at the most convenient times for you. Calculating what is best for you and planning the implementation of a strategy that fits you like a glove takes a lot of probing questions, hopefully reading this book should help you ask the right question so that you can work out a seller financing plan for you and your deal.

3 - WHY WOULD ANYONE DO IT?

England is a place steeped in tradition and there is a cultural reluctance to try anything new or to do things differently to the standard way without the backing of a well-known institution.

So why would you lend money to someone who is buying from you?

Financing someone to buy from you is often called *becoming the bank* and the UK has had a good run at being the banking capital of the world. Until the credit crunch most people would consider banking to be a good profitable business to be in, just ask HSBC.

Still, the question remains *WHY would you do it?* Well the first thing to consider is exactly that, the Credit Crunch. It means, for many reasons it is harder now to borrow money. 1. The lending criteria for loans has become much stricter. 2. The lenders have less money and don't want to get caught short.

(This is not an exhaustive list, just a couple of examples to illustrate my point.)

If you are selling a property, the amount of people who can actually complete on a purchase has been dramatically reduced. The idea that you can buy any property and it will shoot up in value, then a few years later you will have made "loads of money" and you can buy something that you actually like have gone. The result is you have a lot less buyers looking, and even less that can follow though all the way to cash in your bank account.

The laws of supply and demand, say supply is high (there are lots of sellers) and demand is low (there are a lot less buyers who can get a mortgage and even less that have the cash). The effect of this means the advertised price goes down (that is the price of your property) and no one wants to pay the advertised price. We are in a recession and expecting a double dip! (At the time of writing)

If you buy a property you want to be able to tell your friends, family and anyone who will listen that you got a great bargain, and if you are paying REAL CASH (no mortgage) well then that discount needs to be very significant.

This however works both ways. The supply of owner-financed properties is very limited; they therefore sell for a higher price. There will not be any discounting; the reality is that they can sell for a premium. When was the last time you dictated terms to your bank? EXACTLY!

This is not a license to rip people off (for that you require a full banking license) you can however expect to get the full value of your property plus compounded interest, paid monthly on your investment.

What do I mean?

A standard 25year repayment mortgage on a £100,000 loan amortised over 25 years at 4% which is a very good rate at the moment. Will result in the borrower paying back a total of £160,029 on a loan of £100,000 and that is for people with the best credit.

If you have a property to sell, wouldn't you like all or even just some of that extra money that the buyer paid because they did not have all the cash to pay you upfront?

When you become the bank and offer seller finance, you can get the full price for your property plus interest for lending the buyer money. This can provide you with a very nice income in your retirement if you are downsizing for example or can be used for inheritance planning.

The length of the loan term and the interest rate is up to you and it is secured against a property that you know better than any bank. You do not have to lend the full purchase price either or wait 25 years for your money, strategies and tax planning are covered in later chapters.

4 - SELLER FINANCING IN BUSINESS

Seller financing is common practice in business at all levels, where you are most likely to notice it is in small business sales.

When looking at small businesses for sale in magazines, the papers or websites, you will frequently see "significant loans for qualified buyers" and often the seller will not charge interest on the loan.

Small businesses, especially sole traders are run to reduce taxes; they will show maximum expenses and minimum profit. If it is your intention to borrow money to purchase such a business, the reduced profit can result in the accounts showing insufficient profits to qualify for the level of debt required to complete a purchase.

When reviewing a small business's accounts, it can seem hard to justify the valuation and even harder to show how the business can cover the loan repayments.

Therefore a lender will want some other security and for the borrower to show an alternative source of consistent reliable income.

All of these factors reduce the number of potential buyers for the business.

By offering seller financing, the seller can get a better price for their business, they can make up for any discounts in price with interest charges on the loan.

The fact is businesses are not the easiest thing to sell, especially if your accountant has been particularly successful in minimizing the profits. A very good successful business can look uneconomical to finance or be virtually impossible to finance. By offering a good financing package to a potential buyer many financing issues can be overcome.

Capital gains are no longer an issue with the new 10% rate up to 1 million but they can be and they used to be.

However, inheritance planning still remains a concern and retirement income all play a part in deciding to offer seller finance.

When buying a business the accuracy and reliability of the accounting information of the seller is a concern. Many sole traders have cash income that is off the books and therefore they cannot prove a single penny, but they still want to get paid for the added value of that income. Unfortunately as a buyer, you only have their word for it.

There are many places a small business can have an unrecorded value where the owner benefits from perks and bonuses that are hard to monetise, but they still want to be compensated for handing them over to the new owner.

A solution can be to retain some of the purchase price for a period of time mutually agreed by both buyer and seller, until certain performance indicators have been reached or financial information has been verified.

If the new owner has not paid in full, then as the previous owner you will want to earn interest on the money that has been withheld.

Owner financing can be a guarantee of performance, the opportunity to get full value for your business, maximise on your selling opportunity by earning interest on your payments.

Proceeds could go to a family member or be paid overseas, the options can seem endless.

As with any loan, you will want to qualify the buyer; this is explained in detail in chapter 9. Basically you must do your best to ensure you are going to get paid before you issue the loan.

It is wise to check the destination of your train before you get on it and most certainly before it leaves the station.

Although I have focused on small business sales, as I mentioned in the beginning, seller finance is used up and down the scale. Many medium and large business sales have transactions that include an element of seller finance. Although it does not work with a hostile takeover, even public companies have been bought that way.

Company buying strategies are much more varied and flexible than property buying strategies and so they deserve more than one dedicated book. There for they are only covered briefly here to illustrate the wide use of seller financing for business sales.

5 - SELLER FINANCE IN PROPERTY

Well this is what this book is really about. You financing the sale of your property and making a healthy profit.

The first thing to point out is that not all your potential buyers will have bad credit and a lack of or no deposit. This is why I am starting with how you can structure a property deal for a buyer with good credit and a good deposit.

In the first example the property is valued at £250,000 and the buyer has £25,000 deposit however that is only 10%. The buyer has a small business and pays tax on a profit of £10,000 per annum they also have an additional £40,000 per annum of cash income from the business. They have approached several banks that were only willing to lend up to £40,000 plus the deposit a total of £65,000 as the buyer was not able to provide 3 years accounts or sufficient proof of income.

A monthly mortgage payment of £1200 would be very close to the rental value for the same property except in this case we have a owner instead of a tenant. Choosing a principle and interest mortgage also known as a "repayment" mortgage at 5.5%

250,000	Purchase price of new property
25,000	Deposit from buyer
225,000	Seller Financed loan

The same sale could be structured in many different ways here are 4 examples:

250,000	Purchase price of new property
100,000	Deposit paid from sale of previous property
150,000	Seller Financed loan 1st charge on property

250,000	Purchase price of new property
50,000	Deposit paid from equity recovered from repo of previous home
200,000	Seller Financed loan

250,000	Purchase price of new property
25,000	Deposit from buyer
162,500	65% Bank mortgage 1st charge on property
62,500	25% Seller Financed loan 2nd charge on property

250,000	Purchase price of new property
20,000	Deposit from buyer
200,000	80% Bank mortgage 1st charge on property
30,000	12% Seller Financed loan 2nd charge on property

For people who do not live in London here are 2 more examples where the property prices are lower:

100,000	Purchase price of new property
10,000	Deposit from buyer
80,000	80% Bank mortgage 1st charge on property
10,000	10% Seller Financed loan 2nd charge on property

I do not recommend offering seller finance to a buyer who cannot pay a reasonable deposit.

If the deposit is below 10% the risk of default increases substantially, you want as big a deposit as possible, if they have less than 10% I would recommend offering them a "rent to own plan".

What is a reasonable deposit? on a £100,000 property I would want to see 10% and know where the money is coming from i.e. not borrowed money? I need to know that they cannot afford to lose their deposit.

On a £50,000 property I would expect a 15% because the purchase price is so low. On a higher value property £400,000 for example I would be ok with as little as 7% if the buyers were a family and could prove the deposit came from their savings. A single person who could not prove the source of the deposit would indicate a higher risk and I would then want a larger deposit.

Multi-Million pound homes with substantial loans:

1,000,000	Purchase price of new property
45,000	Stamp duty and professional fees (e.g. legal, valuation)
100,000	Deposit from buyer (includes their stamp & fee's)
<u>650,000</u>	65% Bank mortgage 1st charge on property
250,000	25% Seller Financed loan 2nd charge on property

1,000,000	Purchase price of new property
45,000	Stamp duty and professional fees (e.g. legal, valuation)
<u>445,000</u>	Deposit from buyer (includes their stamp & fee's)
600,000	25% Seller Financed loan 2nd charge on property

1,000,000	Purchase price of new property
45,000	Stamp duty and professional fees (e.g. legal, valuation)
245,000	Deposit from buyer (includes their stamp & fee's)
<u>400,000</u>	40% Bank mortgage 1st charge on property
450,000	45% Seller Financed loan 2nd charge on property

2,000,000	Purchase price of new property
90,000	Stamp duty and professional fees (e.g. legal, valuation)
<u>390,000</u>	Deposit from buyer (includes their stamp & fee's)
1,700,000	85% Seller Financed loan 1st charge on property
2,000,000	Purchase price of new property
90,000	Stamp duty and professional fees (e.g. legal, valuation)
<u>690,000</u>	Deposit from buyer (includes their stamp & fee's)
1,400,000	70% Seller Financed loan 1st charge on property
2,000,000	Purchase price of new property
90,000	Stamp duty and professional fees (e.g. legal, valuation)
490,000	20% Deposit from buyer (includes their stamp & fee's)
<u>1,200,000</u>	60% Bank mortgage 1st charge on property
400,000	20% Seller Financed loan 2nd charge on property

Having qualified your buyer, we must look at your situation and objectives to be able to plan the proposed financing. What are your reasons for offering seller finance? Is your objective to sell the property at a higher price? Or to increase the number of buyers who can afford your property by reducing the amount of bank financing that they will require?

Maybe you are lending to provide yourself with a steady income in retirement? This would offer you a much higher rate of return than a savings account. Perhaps you want to provide an income for a family member as part of an inheritance strategy? Or have you exceeded your one million pound windfall tax allowance?

Do you own multiple properties that would be subject to capital gains tax? Have you provided finance as a long term tax efficient offshore strategy? Alternatively the property is already owned by an offshore company or trust and traditional financing is expensive, limited, inefficient, cumbersome or requires considerable disclosure to arrange, given your holding structure.

Seller financing is far from being just for borrowers with bad credit. Seller Finance can be very quick, a smart, cost effective and highly profitable strategy for buyers and sellers in all income brackets and property values.

Traditional financing offers lower loan to value ratios than personal financing when buying using a company, you might want to buy a property or land for development. Short-term seller financing could make all the difference to the margins to get the deal done.

Here is an example of how you could finance a property for development:

£600,000   Value of derelict property in current condition
£250,000   Cost of renovation work

The end value is expected to be £1,200,000 the developer has £90,000 deposit.

£600,000   Value of derelict property in current condition
£ 90,000   Deposit
£240,000   40% Development loan 1st charge
£270,000   45% Seller finance mortgage 2nd charge

6 - FINANCING STRATEGIES AND STRUCTURE

My 11 favorite strategies:
Maximum sale price

Short term high yield interest only (balloon payment)

Medium term with a balloon payment

Cash now, cash in the middle and cash later

Long term income (early repayments penalty)

Stepped payments

Stepped interest only

Stepped interest and principle (low start mortgage)

Developer special

Developer special with long-term finance.

Developer JV (underwriting the development)

Maximum sale price

How to get the maximum selling price – first you should get a quote from 3 estate agents take the 3 prices and if they are reasonably close, pick the middle price. If they are wildly different get more quotes and then average out the closer quotes excluding any quote that is way higher or lower. This is how you calculate your base price, your starting point. Even if you use the lowest price you will still end up with more money because of the interest that you charge on the loan.

Quote 1 - £220k   Quote 2 - £200k   Quote 3   - £230k

Your sale price £220,000

Next I will show you how, even if you sold at £200k, you would still make more than £230k because of the interest.

£200k   Price for example (I however recommend you go with £220k)
£ 20k   Deposit (they will also need some money for stamp duty and fees)
£120k   60% mortgage from a standard lender
£ 60k   30% Seller finance at 8%

The total paid to you on the loan over 25 years would be £140,517

The buyer would pay you 300 monthly payments of £468.39 after 25 years you would have received a total of £280,517 for your house :o)

Short term high yield interest only (balloon payment)

This is a good strategy to use when the buyer can demonstrate to you that they have funds coming in from another source for example the sale of another asset (business, property or other).

£200k   Property sale price
£ 20k   Deposit (they will also need some money for stamp duty and fees)

£180k   90% Seller Finance at 9.5% for up to 18 months would be similar to bridging finance. Payments of £1425pm followed by the £180k balloon payment. If the buyer took the whole 18 months you would earn £25,650 in interest. If they had to get a bridging loan the interest would be higher and they would have set up fees, exit fees and legal fees making the total cost much higher.

Medium term with a balloon payment

A good use for this strategy is when you are happy for the loan to run for a few years but you do not want to be committed to a long-term loan.

£200k   Property sale price
£ 20k   Deposit (they will also need some money for stamp duty and fees)
£120k   60% mortgage from a standard lender
£ 60k   30% Seller finance at 8% for 6 years with a balloon payment

The total interest paid over the 6 years would be £28,800

The buyer would pay you 72 monthly payments of £400 after 6 years you also get your balloon payment of £60k and in total would have received £228,800 for your house

Cash now, cash in the middle and cash later

A good fit for this strategy is when the buyer has a large deposit, a deposit that is not immediately available or they earn large end of year bonuses but do not meet all the criteria for high street lending.

£200k   Property sale price
£ 20k   Deposit (they will also need some money for stamp and fees)
£130k   65% Seller finance 1st charge at 5.5% or as a tracker mortgage
£ 50k   25% SF 2nd charge at 9% for 5 years with a balloon payment

Cash now - you sell the house and get an initial deposit of £20k then you have 2 loan payments coming in of £595.83 & £375. Cash in the middle - as and when the buyer receives the lump sums of funds they are expecting. The buyer can reduce the balance of the 2nd charge loan at any time, however at the end of the 5 year term the balloon payment becomes due and they must settle in full. Cash later - if the loans run their full terms you will receive £178,749 on the 1st loan and £22,500 on the 2nd and that is just the interest, the grand total would be £401,249 for a £200k house.

Long term income (early repayments penalty)
This can be a great retirement income strategy
£200k   Property sale price
£ 40k   Deposit (they will also need some money for stamp and fees)
£160k   80% Seller finance 1st charge at 5.5% or as a tracker mortgage

With this strategy you would receive monthly payments of £733.33 from an interest only mortgage, resulting in you receiving a total of £419,999 providing they do not settle the loan early. To discourage early repayment I would recommend, that as the interest rate is fixed for the term, you should demand a payment equal to 5 years interest in the first 5 years. Then a payment equal to 2 years interest thereafter for the term if you use a low fixed rate. These terms would be unreasonable if it was a high rate of interest. The low interest rate makes the penalty reasonable. The terms may seem harsh but you can expect more stringent terms amongst high street lenders offering long term fixed rates.

Stepped Payments

A great strategy that you can use to provide your borrower with a low initial monthly payment, Additionally it acts as an incentive to refinance in the future or a penalty for failing to meet a deadline for payment.

The basic element is that the amount of the payment increases at pre-set time periods, this is similar to how a credit card works in that the minimum payment reduces the outstanding balance very slowly or it can mean that the loan balance increases over time.

Stepped payments must be planed carefully and used wisely otherwise the buyer can become trapped as has been known to happen with credit cards. However with the right plan you can help your buyer and make a bigger profit in the process, here is a example:

£200k Price for example
£ 20k Deposit (they will also need some money for stamp and fees)
£120k 60% mortgage from a standard lender
£ 60k 30% Seller finance at 8% amortised over 25 years

At 8% the buyer should be paying you £468.39 but they also have the £709pm for the bank loan on the £120k you could reduce their monthly payment to say £200pm in the first year and increase the payment by £50 each year until you reach the full payment. The unpaid portion of the payment would then be added to the loan each month and then incur interest. The amortisation schedule is fairly complex to calculate but you need to do this so the buyer and your self will very clear how much extra this will cost them. By the end of the first year their loan balance would have increased by £3220.68 that they would then be charged 8% interest on in subsequent years.

Stepped Interest Only
When you step the interest, the payment is reduced because you are charging less for the loan, not deferring payment. The key difference here is that the balance will not be increasing over time.

A 60k loan at 4% is £200pm, then at 5% £250pm, 6% £300pm, 7% £350, 8% £400, 9% £450 and so on. In this case you may agree that the interest rate is 6% for the first year then increases 1% per year annual until you reach 9% and then it is fixed until settled.

Stepped Interest and Principle (low start mortgage)

When you step the interest and principle together it provides the borrower with the opportunity to reduce the balance of the loan during the reduced payment stage. This can be a great incentive to pay the loan off early before the cost increases.

Developer Special

When you have a property that requires major works, using this strategy can make a significant increase on what you get paid and how many buyers are interested. Often a development project can be hard to finance because less lenders operate in that market and they want lower loan to value ratio's the effect is the developer needs to have a lot more money available to complete the project. When you provide seller finance as a developer loan this will make your project a lot more attractive, here is how it can work.

Your property is valued a £200k in it's current condition. At cost of £60k a developer can turn your house in to 2 flats worth £180 each, but that means they need at least £265k to do it. You can take a small deposit for example 20% and lend the developer the balance with token or no payments until completion of the works and sale or refinance.

£200k Property value in current condition

£ 40k Deposit

£160k Seller Finance loan at 9% stepped by 1% every 3 months payments deferred for the first 12 months, you could have the developer pay you £100pm from the beginning of the loan to keep them in the habit of paying you. The stepped interest acts as a penalty for delays completing the works. The first 6 months makes you £7,200 interest the following 3 months £3999 the following 3 months £4398 so it is in the developers interest to complete the project as fast as possible. Remember you adjust the terms to your deal.

Developer Special with long-term finance.

Some development projects do not work well with short term financing or they may require a mix of short and long-term finance. For this I recommend a combination of the developer special previously explained and the standard long term seller finance strategies I outlined earlier.

Developer JV (underwriting the development)

Partnering with a developer can prove very profitable, but you do not want to take on all the risk or have the risk passed to you bearing all the costs. When you own the property in a developer joint venture you want to protect yourself against being left with a half-finished project.

An easy way of doing this is to sell the developer a 50% share in your property and seller finance their purchase using the Standard Developer Special Structure, with stepped interest as a penalty for failing to complete within an agreed time frame. On completion you have a choice to make - Sell on the property and get standard commercial funding and so recover some of your equity or seller finance the development on to the end buyer.

This might be a good time to realise some of your profits by taking a substantial deposit or only offering finance as a 2nd charge based on the end purchaser finding a commercial lender willing to take a first charge on the completed development. When structuring a developer special or developer JV always insure that the developer has financial risk other than the redevelopment costs. If you don't you may find if things go wrong that your partner has no real motivation to resolve the issue in a timely manner and therefore only you would suffer.

7 - LAW & TAX

This chapter is a basic guide to some of the major issues and possible solutions. I am not a solicitor nor an accountant and even if I was, your individual state of affairs varies significantly. Your action plan needs to be tailored to your unique opportunities in order to produce the best possible outcome. Key factors such as continually evolving legislation and the chancellor's latest budget can have a considerable impact on the profitability of your loan. The chancellor's budget will present new opportunities but often makes previous strategies less desirable or no longer applicable.

There are some basic but important issues that you should be aware of when you are structuring a loan. It is essential that you get up to date legal advice to ensure that your loan agreement is compliant with current UK laws and enforceable within HM courts. Good tax advice is also vital in order to keep the extra money you have earned.

In the UK, financial services and the provision of advice regarding those services is regulated by the FSA. This includes loans, mortgages, banking, insurance and many other related activities.

The FSA issues licences to carry out regulated activities. Unfortunately obtaining a license is often expensive, slow and requires that you under-go training. Additionally, each license limits you implicitly to that specified activity. It is important that you keep your activities within the guidelines of what you can legally do.

Unless you are a licensed mortgage advisor it is a criminal offence to give mortgage advice. When you offer seller finance you should not advise the borrower unless you are licensed to provide mortgage advice by the FSA.

The easiest way to make money with seller finance is to avoid doing anything that is either regulated or requires you to be licensed.

Things to avoid:
Do not give mortgage advice
Do not issue regulated mortgages

Regulated mortgages

The FSA has categorised loans meeting a specific criteria as regulated mortgages. Naturally, to issue regulated mortgages, you must become a FSA licensed mortgage lender. Should you create a loan that matches the criteria of a regulated loan and not be licensed to do so, the loan will then be deemed null and void. The borrower would not be required to make any payments.

A loan is considered a regulated mortgage when:

The borrower plans to occupy more than 30% of the property as their residence.

The lender has secured their loan as a first legal charge against the property.

Examples of unregulated loans would be when the loan is secured by a second charge or the borrower has no intention of living in the property. Buy to let mortgages and commercial premises are examples of where the borrower has no intention of living in the property and therefore any loans secured on them would be an unregulated loan.

In many countries landlords will sell properties to their tenants with a good payment history, lending the tenant funds towards the purchase. This can result in the landlord having the only or first legal charge against the property. In the UK this would mean the landlord has created a regulated mortgage and would be required to be a licensed mortgage lender.

A possible solution would be for the tenant to receive a primary loan from a licensed mortgage provider and you provided them with additional lending. Even if your loan is more than the primary loan, but then secured with a second and/or a third charge, your loan would be an unregulated loan.

If you lend money as a first charge while works are carried out to a property that the borrower intends to live in but plans to settle your loan with a remortgage before occupying the property that would be an unregulated loan. This is commonly known as bridging finance.

To protect yourself you can write in your loan agreement that the borrower must settle the loan in full before occupation. Thus making occupying the property a fundamental breach of the loan agreement.

The key here is to only offer unregulated loans and a loan is only unregulated when it does not meet the criteria set by the FSA to be a regulated loan. The criteria can be changed by the FSA when they deem necessary one reason of many to instruct legal council to act in your interests.

Loans are income-producing assets and therefore can be treated like any other investment within a pension plan, providing you with a long-term tax-free income. The structure of your loan agreement will affect which taxes and what allowances/exemptions are applicable to you. Again, this is dependant on how the loan is setup.

There are some really clever things that you can do to diminish inheritance tax. Implementing such a complex strategy successfully requires the use of a succession-planning specialist not just a tax advisor. However, because of the substantial amount of money involved it is definitely worthwhile.

8 - SERVICING THE LOAN

Servicing of the loan can often be overlooked until it becomes a problem. You need accurate independent verification of payments and payment history; you should produce statements for the borrower so that both parties are clear of where they stand and the outstanding balance.

Mortgage lenders tend to do annual statements, you can do statements every six months if you prefer. I recommend the annual format stating payment history, amount paid this year, interest rate and outstanding balance.

Clear records help prevent disputes and if there is a disagreement or miscalculation, it will be easy to track and rectify.

Should you choose to sell the loan at some point, independent verification of payment history is essential. A nice easy way to do this is to open up a separate current account to exclusively service this loan with your existing bank. This is similar to the practice of solicitors for client money, which they are required to keep separate from their own funds.

The borrower can pay using a standing order so that the payment date remains consistent. Into an account that you use solely to collect their payments, this means that if you have to produce their payment history to a loan buyer, in court or for the borrower to refinance, you are able to show official bank statements that do not contain your personal banking transactions.

Another option is to use a loan servicing agent, who will collect your payments by direct debit for you. They can run periodic credit checks on the borrower to ensure their circumstances have not changed. They will report the payment history to a credit reference agency making it easier for the borrower to refinance and get credit from other sources. Loan servicing agents will compile the reports for you and the borrower, this independent verification can make it easier to sell the loan should you wish to and all for a small monthly fee.

9 - QUALIFYING THE BUYER

Seller financing is about money! Lots of money! Your money! Thousands! Tens of thousands! Hundreds of thousands and in some cases MILLIONS!!!!

If you want to get paid, you need to do your best to ensure the borrower is able to pay you. Circumstances can change but it is a negligent practice to lend someone money that clearly cannot afford to pay.

Here I will take you through the basic steps of qualifying a buyer, having said that a person is seeking seller finance because of understanding and flexibility. The underlying principle is that you will give them a chance and provide a fair and reasonable opportunity to make a purchase and pay over time. For this, they will pay you a little extra.

Identification, the first point we must cover is that you must know with whom you are dealing with. You must be diligent, you are becoming the bank, you should take a photocopy of their passport and driving license, YOU or your solicitor must make the copies from the original.

If the applicant is a foreign national, and the passport is in another language, you will want an official notarized translation and documentation confirming that they are residing in the country legally and have a valid work permit (that is not expiring any time soon).

For best practice, I would recommend you use the UK's thorough Anti Money Laundering verification document checklist.

You want references and they should be written, yes you must check the references. Confirm it is not a friend or a sister but an employer or a landlord. I once had someone give me her boyfriend's name to provide me with a reference, she said its ok he's an accountant, now that is unacceptable! A good reference is an official who has known the applicant for more than 1 year in a professional capacity and willing to put in writing that the person is reliable and trustworthy and other comments suggesting they are of good character.

You must see their credit report, you need to know how financially stable they are. You need to know what other debts they have and if they can afford the payments. Just because someone is interested and /or would prefer a seller financed deal does not mean they have bad credit.

If your buyer has a poor credit history, you need to know. This should affect the structure of your deal. You will need to take into account the higher risk of default and that your loan would have a lower value if you try to sell it.

If a buyer has credit issues you need to listen to them and understand their situation to make a good lending decision. Remember what kicked off the credit crunch, greed and bad lending decisions.

If someone cannot afford the rates for people with good credit, charging them a higher rate because no one else will accept them just means that you are going to get to share in their financial worries later on.

There are people whose income is inconsistent, people who earn a low basic income and get cash payments that can be difficult to prove. The self-employed and business owners with poor record keeping or who have an income on the books that is much lower than they actually take home.

Listen to their explanations. Caring for a seriously ill relative or going through a divorce can have a negative impact on their credit history.

Often people get in to problems because they allowed a partner to take out credit in their name. Then a breakdown in the relationship results in the partner refusing to pay, this then shows up on their credit report. Disputed payments with suppliers such as catalogues or mobile phone companies, another common source of trivial damage.

Credit reports are a minefield and frequently contain many errors. Mistakes on a credit report are often difficult to correct. Additionally, there are many ways genuine 'negative information' is displayed without context, unfairly damaging your potential buyers' credit history.

These are all valid reasons that financial institutions behavioral scoring systems will not take in to account, but you can.

Financial institutions use behavioral scoring systems to automate decision making in the lending process. Any of the above reasons will cause the systems to decline the potential borrower.

It is up to you to take all the factors into consideration when making your lending decision. Base your decision on facts and personal judgement. Be fair and prudent, but be careful of hard luck stories. By all means give to charity but DO NOT GIVE AWAY YOUR HOUSE that you need the proceeds from just to get the deal done.

Consider the amount you are lending them and how you will get by if they stop paying, how will them not paying affect you and your bills? How much protection from their circumstances do you need? How strong are your finances? If you have to repossess the property, what are the financial implications for you?

Always remember what they tell you in the safety demonstrations on the aeroplane. You must put your own oxygen mask on first before you help others.

It may sound like a nice idea to help the unemployed family with six children and their elderly sick mother but can you afford to pay their mortgage payments for them?

You must make economically sensible business decisions. You can donate 10% of your profits to your favourite charity or 20% if you can really afford it, but do not go bankrupt trying to house people who cannot afford to pay their own mortgage payments.

There are many variations you can do in your seller financing plan to make the payments easier to manage. In planning and strategies you can see how you can change the terms to accommodate a wider variety of circumstances, but do not sign a loan agreement with someone you do not believe can afford it or load a loan in such a way that the interest payments escalate to a point where you know there is no way they can afford to pay it off.

Credit card interest is known for being high with low payments so that when you make the minimum payments it can take you up to 17+ years to pay off £1000. If you design a mortgage with interest like that the borrower will most likely default or at some point in time sue you for an unfair contract.

So to qualify a buyer you must:

Check and verify their identification keeping photocopies of their documentation.

The original loan contract should be kept together with a copy of the buyer's credit report and references.

Proof of income and how they expect to pay you back.

Proof of address, bills i.e. council tax

Check previous addresses match with their credit report.

By gathering this information you can show you have done your best to produce a fair and affordable loan agreement.

Be flexible, your borrower can order a credit report online. Have them do it in front of you (so there is no opportunity to edit the report). We live in a world where identity theft is common place, trust but verify. If things do not add up, do not do the deal, unless you can afford to give away your house.

You are talking about a lot of money, take note of their national insurance number from their pay slips. If they are self-employed, ask for their last tax return, the more money they are borrowing the more you will want to know. Qualifying the buyer is about providing yourself with a sense of security so that you can sleep at night.

10 - THE LOAN AGREEMENT

The loan agreement is one of the 3 fundamentals that are essential for a successful outcome. Lending money without a loan agreement is called a gift, if things work out the way you want them to; you have been blessed with amazing good fortune.

You can get a standard loan agreement from some newsagents or buy one online; however I would not recommend this approach. Can you imagine a major bank using one of these contracts?

They will not have the custom terms you require that make seller financing work for you. When designing your loan agreement you should remember that it needs to work for both the buyer and the seller. Remember credit card companies are having their contracts thrown out of court for being unfair, meaning they are unenforceable. That is people being told by the courts that they legally do not need to repay their loans because of their lenders unreasonable practices.

Your loan agreement needs to be a win win situation for both parties or why sign it? And if they signed it reluctantly the other party will put as much effort as possible into finding the holes in it to get out of it.

So write up what you would like to have in your agreement as early as possible so you can give it a lot of consideration. Then, when you meet the other party you can use these suggestions as a guide to how the contract could be.

Only when you have both parties can you work out the points that make the loan agreement a win/win. In practice you should take your time and write up an agreement, both take it away, think about it, then having given it some thought, you can refine it.

When you have reached a final draft as to what you would like to see in the contract, you should then as a seller have a solicitor draw up the agreement for you. The guide as to what should be in the loan agreement is called a 'Heads of Terms' and once you have it you can send your 'Heads of Terms' to your solicitor to make it a legally compliant contract that will be binding on both parties.

The clearer your instructions to your solicitor, the less your fees will be, so be reasonable and ensure both parties are happy and clear, then you will have a lot less back and forth with your solicitor.

It is worth remembering, a well-structured loan can be sold if you need money in a hurry. A solicitor can advise you on making your loan agreement legally compliant and enforceable should it become necessary.

Making your loan agreement a win-win for both parties should make it unnecessary to use legal means to enforce or collect your money. To make your loan saleable, you need to talk to a loan buyer or broker as to their requirements.

11 - ADVANCED STRATEGIES

By now you should have a solid understanding of seller finance, the benefits and the risks. You maximise the benefits and reduce the risks by creating a tailor made solution that creates synergy between buyer and seller. All too often people are in a rush to close a deal without taking the time to really understand the needs and desires of both parties.

Advanced strategies are about going all the way to get an amazing solution that makes life so much better for both sides. This has the effect of both increasing the benefits and dramatically reduces the risk of default.

You have a property that needs immediate work of substantial value or the property is in such a state that it does not meet mortgage criteria e.g. it has no kitchen or bathroom.

Solution: Except a low deposit from buyer with proof of funds for the works to be carried out on the property. Set a time frame for works with discounts and penalties for performance. Discounts and penalties should only be applied on the backend after completion so as not to make it harder for the buyer to complete the works.

As a seller you want to get a high price for your property without having to do any building work and you want a financial cushion from the buyer.

12 - ALTERNATIVES

Seller Finance is an extremely flexible strategy for selling or buying a home, property or business and can be used for selling or buying most high value items.

There are however circumstances when it is not the most suitable option. A good example of this is when there is a very high risk of buyer default such as with little or no deposit. When contemplating any deal, to set you up for success, make sure the balance of probability is on the side of the deal working out for everybody in the long term.

Sometimes there is no deal to be had, so be prepared to investigate the options and walk away if you are unable to make it work for all sides. If your buyer does not have your required deposit they are alternatives that may be a better fit.

Rent to own / lease option
A great way to sell a property to a buyer you believe can follow through but has little or no deposit is a rent to own plan.

You can accept a small payment, normally 3% of the purchase price. This is called consideration for doing the deal; it is not a deposit but an incentive for you to agree to the terms. They will then pay you the market rent plus an extra payment in exchange for your agreement to allow them to purchase the property in the future for a price fixed now. This 'option' to purchase can last for a number of years 2,3,4,5 sometimes even more the decision is yours.

The tenant rents the property from you until they decided to exercise their 'option to purchase' or the agreement expires. You may choose to offer them a discount on the purchase price based on the consideration they have paid you.

Remember the money they pay you is not a deposit. If you accept a deposit legally you would have entered in to an installment contract and/or given the tenant equity in your property before they have exercised the option to purchase. If they default on the rental payments and you have to evict them from the property by excepting a deposit you will have given them 'equitable interest' this means you made them a part owner of your property changing a simple eviction in to a repossession hearing and a legal nightmare for you.

Your intention should be to help them get in to a financial position that they can buy your home, not create a legal nightmare for yourself. The payments you except are for the sole purpose of agreeing to sell the property in the future at a price you have set now.

Another option would be to place the property in to a trust where upon completion the beneficiary will change to the new owner. This is similar to a hire purchase agreement, in that until they have made the final payment you remain the owner or the trust's beneficiary. This is complex to set up and they are nearly always better alternatives, so think carefully about placing a property in a trust just to sell it.

Mortgage wrap

A wraparound mortgage is when you sell a property 'subject to' existing finance. This however normally breaches the terms and conditions of the existing loan, specifically the 'due on sale' clause the lender can now demand payment in full of the outstanding balance, should they become aware of the sale. Repossessing the property if they do not receive immediate payment in full.

Traditionally lenders have not acted in this manor providing payments where not in arrears and kept up to date. However times have changed and the financial positional of the lender will be the most significant factor, if repossessing the property will help them or their current cash flow that is what they will do.

So this remains a very risky option but it can be made to work in some circumstances, if you are selling to a family member who you would be willing to make their payments for them should the occasion arise. Remember the finance is still in your name and you are still solely responsible and if you fail to pay it will affect your credit. When you take these factors in to account if you are happy to do it all the lending is already in place, all they have to do is make the payments.

Mortgage assignment

In some cases a lender maybe willing to allow another party to take over the payments to your existing mortgage. This would be an assignment of the loan payments or an assumption of the loan depending on how the paperwork is done; in the UK this will only be possible in very rare circumstances. From the lenders point of view why would they want to release the original borrower from the loan contract?

They are however cases where the lender may see this as an advantage, so do not rule it out. An example of this could be that the property is in negative equity and they will lose money by repossessing the property and even though they can go after the borrower for the short fall for the next 12 years they are unlikely to be able to recover the full amount.

If the case is that by allowing for the assignment of the mortgage they will gain a new party whom is a good lending risk and willing to pay the full loan value or close too there is now an incentive for the lender to agree to the assignment of the loan. A new loan would result in the property being re-valued which may not be in the interests of the lender or borrower. You can of course just assign the payments but this will have the same hazards of a mortgage wrap.

Commercial lending can often be assigned or assumed by a new party subject to the approval of the lender.

ABOUT THE AUTHOR

Paul is a serial entrepreneur having started many business and is always quick to tell you how he eats, sleeps, reads and practices on a daily basis.

Having spent the last 10 years in property with a heavy focus on the financing side, his knowledge of creative finance has saved many a deal and landlord.

Currently he offers structured finance consultancy, bridging finance and a "Done For You" seller finance service in partnership with a prominent law firm. Their services include: Writing loan agreements, providing loan tax advise, succession planning, loan servicing and conveyancing.

To find out more visit:
www.AboveMarketValue.co.uk

18494276R00030

Printed in Great Britain
by Amazon